Clear a Place for Good

NEW POEMS 2006 – 2012

By

HANS OSTROM

Clear a Place for Good

NEW POEMS 2006 – 2012

By

HANS OSTROM

© 2012 by Hans Ostrom. All rights reserved.

Congruent Angle Press

First edition.

ISBN-13: 978-0-9844175-4-4

ISBN-10: 0-9844175-4-0

Many of the poems in this book appeared previously on the blog, *Poet's Musings* (http://poetsmusings-muser.blogspot.com/). I recorded several for the Youtube channel, *langstonify*.

"Message From a Bookmark" was published in a limited edition as a bookmark by the Collins Press. Grateful acknowledgement.

Black Ice, KONCH, and ***Writing on the Edge*** are among the magazines in which some of these poems were previously published. Thanks to the editors.

Thanks as well to friends and family members, writers who have taken classes from me, and writers & readers in communities where I have lived and worked.

Cover illustration and book design by Mike Martin. Author photo by Nathan Aune. Logo design by Rob Beezer.

For Jackie and Spencer

Table of Contents

Mere Sympathy 9
Transaction 10
Crushing Fate 12
Modernist Shame 14
Nostalgia for Nothing 15
Labor Breaks 16
Only Dreaming 17
Light Verse 18
Democracy Today 20
Of Photosynthesis 21
Chocolate 22
Human in an Airport 24
Message From A Bookmark 25
Sexual Orientation 26
When the Tongue 27
The Cunnilingus Poem 28
Go As You Wish 33
Dice 34
Channel-Crossing 35
Idiosynchronized 36
Villanelle: The Villain, L 38
Civil Liberties Sonnet 39
Quantum Sonnet 40
Novel: A Sonnet 41
Cosmic Status 42
Nub of the Matter 43
Wary Lyric 44
Oh Ballad, Dear Ballad 45

Duke Ellington..46

Ballad of the Micro-Town 48

Langston Hughes and Barack Obama 49

Blogosonnet..50

El Greco's *Christ on the Cross* 51

For the Birds...52

Skin-Scanner 53

Skin's Stars 54

A Wave in San Diego 55

Like a Simile, As a Sign 56

The Compost-Lesson..57

Evangelical Detour...58

Retired Oracle 60

For Librarians 61

Insurance..63

Rampant Significance 64

The Clothing...65

Any Storm in the Port 66

Clear a Place for Good..67

How to Get Ideas for Poems 68

How to Write a Poem 70

Before Katrina 71

Phantom Pantoum 72

Sonnet in a Bar 73

Molecular Mood 74

Salongen och Skogen..75

Polite Society Versus the Woods 75

Critic 76

Door Poem 77

Elsewhere	78
Woman in a Waiting-Room	79
Worrisome Quatrain	80
August Afternoon	81
Horizon	82
Strong Views	84
Horse-Trail, High Sierra	86
Poem by the Side of the Road	87
Highest Form of Art	88
A Writer of Parables	89
Fleeting Real	90
Bear Nearby	91
Moon-Shot 1969: the Missing Article	92
Man in a Hole	93
Sestina: The Game of Baseball	94
Memo From November 6th Street	96
Memphis Monologue	98
Adjustment Denied	99
A Little Something That Refrains	100
Because Comparisons Matter	101
The Time-Drunk	102
Chardin's *Still Life With Fish*	104
If I Were a Werewolf	105
Celebrity Author	106
His Photos Were Not His	107
Oakland Is There	108
Old Seagull	109
Rhinoceros	110
About Hobbema's Landscape	111

Towards Evening	112
Small Garden	113
The River Moved	114
Spuds	115
No Strings Attached	116
Mongrel	117
Employee	118
Lyric Craving	119
Venues	120
Rhododendrons Without a Country	121
For Cafeteria Workers	122
Watching Bach Played	123
The Ambitionator	124
The Fallibility Sonnet	125
Notes in Five Paragraphs on How to Write an Essay	126
They Say About a Poem	128
Walk in the Sunshine	129
Crossing the Creek	130
In One Quiet Room	131
Evening Hatch	132
Still Surprised	133
Intimacy	134
The Extravagance and Reticence of Love	135
Into the Folds of It	136
Index of First Lines	*137*
Index of Titles	*140*
About the Author	*143*

Mere Sympathy

I'm feeling sorry for yourself.
I bring some empathy to your shelf

of discomfort. It's such a small
gift, sitting there against the wall.

I wonder if it does you any good.
Guilt gets me thinking that I should

convert it to fuel which would power me
to cook, transport, listen; to see

to something that might lessen pain;
to soothe, repair, or entertain:

something, anything, specific for you,
that is, as opposed to

this general sympathetic feeling,
which hangs above us like a ceiling.

∎

Transaction

Although we've never met
and odds are never will, we
virtually converge here on line 3.
I left imagery home
because I wanted to meet you
unspecifically as I write and you
read this. I figured you wouldn't
want to be imagined, for you
already exist. You are who

you are, not what anyone
says you're like: oh, if that

were only true. Similitude
is difference with a mask on.
What happens next is that
you think what you will
inside your life, mind, body,
moment. You are the only

you you'll ever be, a verifiable
rarity. It is good to meet you
here without having to know you,
and there's a good chance you may
feel the same. Your reading this
transactional poem is what the poem
will be. You complete it by being there

and here. Reading, you finish the poem
I'm about to finish—none too soon.

In poetry, this qualifies as business
transacted. It's been a pleasure doing
language with you.

∎

Crushing Fate

"People who believe that they are strong-willed
and masters of their destiny can only continue to
believe this by becoming specialists in self-deception."
  — James Baldwin, *Giovanni's Room*

Once someone advised me to run
to my fate and crush it in my arms.
He may have been confused about what
fate is, who's the crusher, and who's

the crushee. Anyway, he confused me,
so I crushed him in my arms. I said,
"I'm practicing." He found my behavior
unpleasant, the bear-hug inappropriate.

As fate had it, we didn't become friends.
—Even if I were to run to my fate, odds
are I'd take off in a wrong direction.
Anyway, I decided I shouldn't go around

pretending it's possible to crush fate
with my arms or with rented fate-
crushing equipment. Some days, I have
trouble just making it to work on time. I'm

in no position to fantasize about crushing
fate—or to give fate-related advice. If
your situation's different, then I say this:
more fate-crushing power to you. If you've
located your fate and are running
toward it now, I give you no assistance.

I wish you good speed, God's
luck, and above all, strong ribs.

∎

Modernist Shame

A student asks some simple questions
of Modernists, of canonical tycoons
such as Eliot and Pound, Rexroth,
William Carlos Williams,
Amy Lowell, and Wallace Stevens:

Why didn't you write about Jim Crow?
Why didn't you include images of lynching
in your Images? Why didn't your art
confront the core savagery of your
American civilization? Your

"achievements," as my professors
call them, are as nothing in the face
of what you chose to ignore, therefore
support. *Dare to eat a peach? Crowds
on London Bridge? Much depends on
a wheel barrow?* Much depended,
literally, from Southern trees. Brown fog
of London is nothing compared to
stench of a burned body.
You can shove your peach.

A goddamned jar in Tennessee? Are you
fucking kidding me, Mr. Stevens? And
I read that letter, the student says,
in which you wrote, "coons in
Ethiopia." You, you Modernists,

your work lards anthologies I'm
asked to buy. You didn't see
them as people, did you? You
didn't see their catastrophe as
your catastrophe.

■

Nostalgia for Nothing

The things I don't remember
about childhood are ones
I miss the most: nights I

slipped quickly into untroubled
sleep, pine-boughed days through
which I tumbled and pretended—
I'm just guessing here. How exotic

the town of Childhood seems.
To think: I once lived there, or so
I tell me. Childhood's a village
with its own sun and moon,

a silver silo full of languid days,
and a golden clock-tower. It is
a place filled with people
who passed on from here,
and what I don't remember
I've grown fond of.

■

Labor Breaks

Labor breaks you. When you're young,
you roll through work, your muscles
and bones handling any kind of shit
labor throws your way. Work, though,
stays young forever while you age.

It laughs with you when you're young,
sure. It hits the bars and runs around
town watching you go after what you think
you want. It gets you up in the morning after
nearly no sleep—no problem, you're young.

Then one day you're not young and labor
hasn't aged a night. It grins and shrugs
as if to say, "Nothing personal," and it
starts to hit you with the tools of your trade,
and you know this then: the work you do will
    break you.

∎

Only Dreaming

In this wet city under gray today,
you'll sense how hard and wearily
so many people work. Could be
you'll grieve for grinding toil
demanded and surrendered. You
might think about how the nation
is always and forever at war,
about the killing and the trauma.
Or maybe you won't have time to
feel much because you're working.

Later you'll get across the city
somehow as gray becomes night.
Inside where you live, you'll note
again how much you and your clothes
smell of the work you do. Now other
tasks await: to cook, to listen,
to worry, to count, to try to rest.
Only dreaming will seem effortless,
but that's dreaming, which is nothing.

∎

Light Verse

So is light particle or wave
or both or neither? I guess
it's principally indeterminate.
Anyway, I read about this
topic a few times using my
bedside light, the bulb lurking
behind a translucent shade
like the moon behind a pale
patina of clouds. It took a while,
but the sun produced Einstein,
for example, and like almost every
other creature, he got thirsty
after walking in sunshine . . . .
Light's the big mystery which teases
its challengers by illuminating
itself with itself, just as God
gave God an order *("Let there
be Be, when You have a minute")*
and followed it to a T . . . If the way,
whatever that is, isn't the truth,
then it will have to do, and it's
a lot easier to find by light—or by touch,
which shines waves and particles on

our brains, too. . . . We say "the power's
out" when we lose our lights, and,
brothers and sisters, that's the truth.
Light's a something from a nothing,
fiat's luxury loping out of *nihilo*.

∎

Democracy Today

A politician's head swelled
and burst out of a televising screen,
crashing onto the floor of my room,
rolling to my feet, where it lay,
face up, a grin glued on like a photo
of a keyboard, eyes fixed wide open,
genderless features painted
with studio-makeup, hair
formed like fine-spun fiberglass,
forehead shining like porcelain.
I howled, jumped up, ran
out the door into the street,
where everyone wore masks
that looked like the face on
the floor of the room I'd fled.
"We're all going to vote!" the
masked crowd cried.
"You will join us!"

■

Of Photosynthesis

Wherever you enter the story,
the story amazes: Single cell
meets ball of fire; epics of
juiced up vegetation ensue—algae,
sequoia, peat, fig, fern, and cacti.

Human history's an offshoot
of photosynthesis, a cud
chewed by divine bovinity
in its green time. When we

entered the story, we cast our
shadows, inserted our names for
plants and stuff, studied and
disrupted processes. Then we grabbed
a green salad for lunch, so busy.

Let scythe or mower,
chainsaw, tiller, test-tube, or gene-
splicer sit for an hour—if
the boss will let you take a break.
Let's lie in wonder under photosynthetic
boughs, yawn our wows amidst
leaf-dappled mottling of light,
and graze on amazement, taking it in.

■

Chocolate

1

After the moon has set but before sunrise,
sweet breezes issue from dark brown corridors
of a warm, fronded forest. This is the hour of
chocolate, when the mind is weary merely
of thinking and wants to dance with ancient
instincts, to self-induce a swoon by
languishing in lore from foreign precincts.

2

Inside cacao beans lies a secret
that survives translations of growth
and harvest, compost, roast and grind,

concoction and confectionery concatenation.
After tasting chocolate, tongues transmit
the news by nerve-line, enzyme,
and bloodstream to mahogany-lined private
clubs in the brain. There receptors
luxuriate on divans and thrill
at the arrival of tropical gossip.
After the messages from chocolate
arrive, brown damask draperies vibrate,
and pleased devotees purr pleasurably.

3

My darling, I wouldn't choose
between chocolates and flowers,
so I brought both. Let me put
the latter in a vase as you open
and taste the former. Yes, I agree:

chocolate is *film noir* watched
by taste buds in the mouth's
art-house theater. Barbarously

suave, chocolate is an unabashedly
debauched foodstuff—cad and coquette
of cacao. Darling, you're making
those noises you make when you eat
chocolate—the secret language of
satisfaction, the patter of pleasure,
your mumbled homage to this,
the moment of chocolate.

■

Human in an Airport

To be human is to sit cross-legged
on a plastic chair at an airport-gate;
to know different meanings
of *gate*; to wear a dark woolen
coat; to wear cotton jeans that owe
their etymology to Genoa; to have had
some of your head's hair tinted yellow
chemically; to wear metal ear-rings;
to wear a diamond-barnacled band
on one finger; to read with great rational,
passionate concentration a book entitled
World War IV; to be one pixel on the screens
of international corporations; and
to mark passages with translucent,
yellow, watery ink as if you
might be personally involved in this
or that denouement of history.
And to sneeze.

■

Message From A Bookmark

If I am in your book, then thanks. Between
The pages, most of me's kept warm. The part
Of me revealed greets you: Where have you been?
This book and I perform our silent art.

∎

Sexual Orientation

First of all, what an unusual term. Second:
during sex, which parts of the body ought
to angle East? Third, if there were a formal
intro to the subject, an
orientation-workshop, what society could
agree about who should lead and take
the course and what topics would be
covered and uncovered? Fourth, people
aren't ships or compasses. They're
people, and desire is a kind of tautology,
a self-evident definition, a personal
concert of emotional music. Fifth, the
sun seems to rise, people have sex, the
sun seems to set, people have sex, and
thus has it been so since so long ago, it
seems like forever. Therefore and sixth,
is it past time to love and let love, to
realize adults young, old, and middling
will find their adult landscapes of desire
using maps that make the most
sense to them and sensing direction from
most idiosyncratic magnets indeed?

■

When the Tongue

When the tongue
touches the perfect
place linguistically
or physically:
an ecstasy,
most certainly.

■

The Cunnilingus Poem

1887 L. C. SMITHERS tr. Forberg's Man.Class. Erotology v. 122 A man who is in the habit of putting out his tongue for the obscene act of cunnilinging. 1897 H. Ellis Stud. Psychol. Sex. I. iv. 98 The extreme gratification is cunnilingus,..sometimes called sapphism.

—*Oxford Dictionary of the English Language,* online

The gratification can be extreme. That's true.
As I look at this poem, I'm feeling good
about it, but we both know that
the poem's language—yes, that's right,
its tongue—oughtn't to degrade, devalue,
pornographize, evade, or abuse its subject.
That's been done. The poem has opened,

chooses telling. Showing happens, too.
The poem does not advise discretion.
It decides to locate itself respectfully where
it believes it's been invited. It chooses to be
human and hopes you'll understand. Now it
proceeds beyond the play of preliminaries.

Her apartment was in a cheap, two-story
stucco heap—palatial compared to my place.

We lay on her bed in a close, hot room: Spring.
California's Central Valley, deep between Coast
Range and Sierra Nevada, had already ovened up.
She kept her window open. She lay back. The
pillow-cases were bright red. She relaxed. She
opened her legs. I went down on her eagerly—I
might say earnestly. Great erotic generosity
inspired me, or so I chose to believe
    about myself.

Wait. There's no rush. We have time to instruct
anatomy, biology, and pornography to go away, to
leave us alone. Believe it or not, this poem
    likes its privacy.

Hot, stuffy, small, and cheap, the room
transformed itself. She and I—well,
we took our time. There was no rush. Our time.
Her room. The heat. I took her own sweet time
and gave some of it back to her.

It was sex. Obviously. We
devoured a ripe, wet, hot interval of
life. That's all and not a little bit. When
she orgasmed (what a mash of syllables),
she seemed to have nothing
to do with the pseudo-scientific infinitive, *to orgasm*.
She screamed. That happens
to be right. Screamed. Yelled
and shouted, too. It was louder for being privately
public. *"Ecstasy"?* I don't know:

That word makes me nervous. It belongs to
romance novels and a drug. There's no rush to
use it. Anyway, her sounds were so loud they startled
me, and I lost my place. I smiled while I was turning *to
cunniling* into a conjugated, tense present. There was
no rush. I found my place again, went back to
     work. Play. It was sex, not poetry.

So far so good? I raised my head
from loving work. It is,
can be, good work—
cunnilingus. It shouldn't be labor
but can be more than play. . . . I
raised my head to listen to her and to
watch the rest of her body and her face

and take in the holy scene of the room. Is
holy too much? Absolutely, so let's leave
it, posted on the stucco heap
like a notice from a landlord. I offered
her a pillow with which to muffle the *aria,*
if she so chose. She chose not so.
Well played! I heard people giggling outside
in California, on the black asphalt of an
apartment-complex's baked parking lot, no rush
of breeze out there. I smiled, and I

went down again into what had become for her a
rich source of satisfaction, a fabled California
mine, a vein of golden pleasure, a rush. I'd
become a famously employed miner, producing
lavish treasure with simple tools, tongue and
mouth and lips. I exhibited care and the will to
give my head. Such a primitive, post-modern
afternoon it was, whatever that means.

It wasn't history,
but it was the best we two could do.
She was the only person she'd ever be.
She wanted to be satisfied on a
rickety bed in a blazing, stucco apartment.
I knew her, and I showed up. I
gave her what she invited me to give.
It was basic and civilized, polite,
profane, sacred, and plain. It tasted and smelled
the way it ought to. She became

immortally satisfied for an interval
of afternoon. I swear I still heard
people laughing at sex-sounds coming,
so to shout, from her open window. I
worked at loving, making a delivery, freighting
freedom and joy to the realm
of her body. That's an overstatement.

I know the names of body-parts,
and so do you. This isn't about that,
but please see references to tongue, lips,
mouth, legs, and head above. The window,
her legs, my mouth, our lives were open.

You can't rush these things, but it
ended. I was a sweating, naked man
with a sense of charity, accomplishment,
and gratitude. And it was fun.
She was a contented naked woman,
so I didn't say anything, and I didn't
want anything. That last bit is a lie.

There's never been a rush to remember,
and it's customary to keep such things
private unless your profession is
pornography or politics. Oh, well, this is a poem,
and poems get interested in this
    kind of thing. You know how it is.

Writing this, I feel good about it.
I smile and pay homage to her ecstasy,
which was different from that word.
She filled herself up. She
shouted, my mouth pressed to her
self-possessed body, which thrilled.
I thrilled at fearsome pleasure. There's

no rush, but one must act. Communion
occurs so variously, mysteriously,
sometimes with stucco and asphalt
nearby, and the rent due. I remember
rubbing my face on her thighs and then
on cotton sheets to get some wet and sweat
off, not all. I licked my lips. I remember
peace, the peace of
a wordless afterwards. No rush, no rush at all. If
this poem offends or bores you, you know why,
and I hope you didn't read this far,
but if you did, it's over now. Be well.

■

Go As You Wish

Go as you wish into that good night.
It's not a night, of course. It's death.
To tell you how to die? I have no right.

Besides, death often hides nearby, plain sight—
Then someone's gone, as quickly as a breath.
Go as you wish into that good night.

Assuming you're allowed your wish, I might
Not even be around, to tell the truth.
To tell you how to die? I have no right.

I've not yet died, nor have I faced the fright
Of certain death, so here's my guess:
Go as you wish into that good night.

I sympathize with D.T.'s rage. That sight
Of one who's dear about to die: *Damn death!*
But still: go as you wish into death's night.
To tell you how to die—I have no right.

∎

Dice

Fold night several times until
it becomes a cube. The North Star
shines on one side, Orion's Belt
on another, and so on. Repeat the

process. You have two cubes.
Now let your fist swallow both
die. Hold your fist high, shake
it against sky defiantly.

Make a wager with God.
Toss the cubes onto
a flat black velvet night. Look
at the way the constellated cubes

have come to rest, inert
and grave. Of course, you've lost.
The House always wins. God is
the House. The rest is a sad casino.

∎

Channel-Crossing

Irish Girl sat on a crate,
topside. Cigarette-smoke
out of her mouth joined
English-Channel mist.
North American Me stood beside
her oafishly. Everyone else
but a bemused British crew
was puking. A man threw up
into the wind. Wet, pink
pebbles flew our way. One hit my cheek.
Below-decks, a *danse-macabre*
of vomiters staggered,
careened. Irish Girl and I
didn't know why we
weren't ill from riding the heaving,
pitching barrel of a boat. Her
smoke smelled fine. I
made her laugh, once only,
can't remember how. Her
eyes were dark blue,
her hair dark brown but
with secret plans to become
red. This was when
the Chunnel was still
a Jungian blueprint beneath
the ocean. We docked, Ostend.
Irish Girl took a train different from mine.
A widening channel of years
later, I do hope she's alive;
never been sea-sick; and laughing.

■

Idiosynchronized

People we see once: flood of faces, coats,
collars—on avenues and plazas, in markets,
theaters, bars, banks, hospitals. A bent

shape hoeing weeds: one of us saw it once
one place one time from a train: This
is an example but only of itself. Its

singularity can't be transposed. Imagine
you remember the person who interested you
terribly in that café that morning that city.

Sure it happened, but you don't remember
because once was not in fact enough. People
we see once are our lives: Forgetting

them (we must), we lose whole arenas
of the lived. Even ghosts return, but not
this vast mass of once-only-noticed

which composes medium and matrix
of our one time here. We are adjacent and
circumstantial to strangers, just one jostle

of flux away from knowing next to everything
about their lives. The river of moments takes
a different channel; the one moment is nothing

now. The once-only appear, then appear to go
to an Elsewhere that defines us. They proceed
to get to know whom they get to know.

Their lives are theoretically real to us, like
subatomic particles. To them their lives
are practically real to them. From their

view, ours are not. We know they were there,
vivid strangers, because they always are,
every day. Like a wreath floating

on the ocean, memory marks a space
abandoned. In large measure life is
recall of spaces occupied. History

consists of someone who insists on being
remembered, someone who insists on
remembering, combinations of both.

Familiarity and routine join to work methodically; they
manufacture things in recall. Vivid strangers
are incidentally

crucial, indigenous to a present moment that is
like a mist over a meadow, rising, evaporating
just when we arrive, past as we are present.

∎

Villanelle: The Villain, L

The villain, L, disrupts this life of ours,
And is, as the imbuer of desire,
A criminal who deftly drains our powers.

Sometimes the villain, L, recedes and cowers,
And lurks as others rush to douse a fire.
The villain, L, disrupts this life of ours.

Is L for Love? For Longing, Lonely hours?
For Lust or Loss? Or maybe just for Liar,
A criminal who deftly drains our powers.

Could it be Language? Our Linguistic powers--
That signifying engine which won't tire?
The villain, L, disrupts this life of ours.

(In many languages other than ours,
A different letter shall be used to hire
A criminal who deftly drains our powers.)

Or L for Light, *fiat-ed* Big-Bang's flowers?
By light, we know and, knowing, we desire.
The villain, L, disrupts this Life of ours,
A criminal who deftly drains our powers.

■

Civil Liberties Sonnet

A civil liberty might be defined
As a chance to have a prayer to defend
Oneself against a power that's aligned
With secrecy and certitude, that's then
Brought out much of the worst in some
Of the cohort who enjoy power, which tends
To unhinge folks. What, however, has been done

Might be undone, with rights restored to mend
The rips in practices that hold a clear
And wary view of power. Checks and rein
And oversights on reign: basic but dear.
Unbounded power just tends to go insane.
Since that's the way it is, that which concerns
Our civil liberties is a priority that burns.

■

Quantum Sonnet

Electrons here, electrons there, but no
Transition anywhere. They disappear.
They reappear—a quantum jump—or so
It's been identified—not well, I fear.

For if the relocation were a jump,
The jumping thing would stay in view.
Electrons don't exactly make a *whump*
When landing after leap. I know it's true

They're ultra-small. Perhaps there is a sleight
Of light in sub-particulated world?
Or maybe God hides in a burst of light—
Photonic God, an energetic whirl

That makes and breaks the rules. Look there
And here, but note an in-between does not appear.

∎

Novel: A Sonnet

There was a place where people lived a long,
Long time. They soaked the place with their despair
and overloaded it with lore and song.
And then one day a stranger traveled there.

His presence was an irritant and salve,
Of course—that dual role which strangers play.
He saw someone and something he *must* have.
His getting them, however, would betray

A secret waiting for him all along.
A certain pressure grew under the weight
of character and fate combined. A wrong
Occurred and love turned into hate.

In more detail, the story stretches out
Three hundred fifty pages, or thereabouts.

■

Cosmic Status

If we add up all that we claim to know,
The sum is zero when compared to Mystery.
We are as nothing in the cosmic show.

Or do you disagree? Maybe it's so
That we are in control, can claim to be,
If we add up all that we claim to know.

If Universe is infinite or so,
Then we're about as trivial as can be.
We are as nothing in the cosmic show.

But if God is, well, then: there you go:
Perhaps God made it all and let us see
If we could claim to add up what we know.

Irrelevant or godly? Hard to know–
A or B? And might there be an option C
In which when we discover all we know,
We're more than nothing in this cosmic show?

∎

Nub of the Matter

I hate to break this news to me:
Logic dictates I don't matter.
Out of not much matter, I am made,
and such matter as I do comprise
does not export significance.

Particles of matter disperse and reconvene
anew. Any one state of particulate
coherence may be lovely (rhododendron
flower, woman's smile) or may be me, whom
I like well enough, but in any case, what
so ensues? In relation to everything,
I'm merest particle of perpetual change.

Only matter can make me. I've already
been made up. Dissolution's penciled in
on a calendar Heraclitus keeps next
to his bedside river of fire. Only God can make
me matter. This is the nub of the matter,
a God's honest truth.

∎

Wary Lyric

I live in wariness,
which is no place.
It is an atmosphere,
a mental space.

Courtesy suggests I
ought to give an image
to sharpen what I mean.
A coyote on a ridge:

It watches, listens, sniffs.
Only hunger makes it vicious.
Otherwise, it lives by wariness,
is naturally suspicious

and alone, even in company.
Me, too, to some degree.
I live in wariness, a type
of fear. That's me.

∎

Oh Ballad, Dear Ballad

"Oh father, dear father,
where did you go?"
"I got drunk and drove
the truck into snow."

"Oh mother, dear mother
why do you cry?"
"'Cause I'm stuck at home
caring for you, that's why."

"Oh grannie, dear grannie
why are you so wise?"
"It's just a *schtick*, kiddo,
like rolling your eyes."

"Oh, God, greatest God,
do you listen to me?"
"You and six billion others,
omnisciently."

"Oh life, dear life,
what should I expect?"
"In good years, a job.
on good days, a check."

■

Duke Ellington

The headline from the *Sacramento Bee*
Announced that Ellington had died. I think
The article may have referred to him as one
Of those things he really was. They got
It right, if I recall: they said he was
"A treasure"—treasure lost to us, to me,
Who'd only just begun to understand
What I'd been blessed to witness when I spent
A few bucks on a ticket for a concert in
A cafeteria—a break from writing essays for
My English 1-B class. I got to hear
Duke Ellington--in a college cafeteria.
That night I was as privileged as a prince
Who'd seen and heard Mozart conduct.
Mere Rocklin was my Salzburg; Duke's jazz,
Demotic classical. Duke Ellington had passed,
The headline said. I thought of him, spot-lit
That night, a black tuxedo, and the hair
Brushed back. That's how he must have looked
As he strolled past Archangel Gabriel.
To Gabe he may have said, "We love you madly—
But try it in a minor key this time."
When I saw him, I was 18 and thought
I knew just what Duke Ellington deserved.
"He's royalty," I thought, "does not deserve
This gig on cold linoleum." Time is

No satin doll who puts her arms
Round you, and now I think I may have learned
What Mr. Ellington believed that he deserved: To
write, to play, and to conduct, as long
as God would let him, and anywhere the bus

Or train or plane might go. The music does
Not know it's in the cafeteria, or in
A segregated Cotton Club. And Mr. Ellington,
It's obvious, could take care of himself.
Ah, heaven's black piano's always tuned.
The A-Train glides like silk into the night.
In Davis, California, and in Harlem, you
Can see the sky, and hear "Mood Indigo."

■

Ballad of the Micro-Town

The mountains round that town are sheer
Massifs of stone. The town
Lies glinting like a coin below.
The river carves a frown.

I grew up there, so it was all.
It was the world to me.
That it and I were less than small
I'd learn eventually.

To have grown up in a small town
Is such a mini-fate,
A shrunken destiny, at best,
A morsel of time's bait.

If you are from a micro-town,
Bravo to you from me.
Our origins have blessed us with
Well known obscurity.

■

Langston Hughes and Barack Obama

Let's lay down some lines for Langston Hughes
this day of news: 20 January 2009. A fine
piece of the dream's no longer deferred,
though the thought's occurred that Mr. Hughes

might focus on the people out of work
or, working, out of money. We must recall
he gave Roosevelt what-for. Still I see
him in a Harlem bar, sitting next to Jesse B.,
speaking in his clipped Midwestern English,
having sipped something fortified,

brown eyes bright and wide.
He'd be smoking if they'd let him, saying
or thinking, 'Lord, a day has come I never even
dreamed to dream in 1921.' He'd go back
to the brownstone with its small garden
in front, sit down, and write a simple,
profound lyric capturing the spirit of
    President Obama's day.

Cross the Jordan, cross the Nile, cross the
Congo—and *that* Ocean, too. Cross the Harlem
and the Hudson Rivers. Cross the Mississippi.
Dear Madame Johnson: Mr. Obama crossed the
Potomac. That's a fact—no not some dream.
Think of Mr. Hughes's rivers. The soul shivers.

■

Blogosonnet

There's nothing spherical about the space
In which innumerable web-logs all appear.
It's just Electronville, the selfsame place
That harbors radio, lightning, and fear.

A universe of language every day
Big-bangs itself into hyper-existence
On billions of screens—a cosmic spray
Of texts that is galactically immense.

The Web is actually a firmament
Of pixelated light. In fact, these blogs
Aren't blogs so much as wee lights meant
To light a billion mental strolls through bogs

Of collective and individual thought:
This is what Gutenberg and Gates hath wrought.

∎

El Greco's *Christ on the Cross*

In El Greco's *Christ on the Cross*, earth
rolls up into sky, which looks like sea—
and it's all one blue-black mass
behind the hanging man who said
his reign was not of this shifty world.

El Greco's Jesus, stuck at the center
foreground, isn't handsome, looks up
exhausted, is almost out of here. A
city's suggested beyond and beneath
nailed feet. It's no city you'd want
to enter. Between the small mound
of bones and limp urban spires, small
men ride tiny white horses. There's

a flag, of course—a standard, which
the painting's enormous blue note
blows away like a dry leaf. Horses
and men seem headed into a lifeless,
lightless cave or copse. Without
a doubt, the flag suggested power
to occupied and occupiers both back then,
as flags are meant to do. El Greco's study's
an indelicate bruise of black-and blue.

■

For the Birds

Here's to starlings
who travel in clouds,
and unsubtle ravens,
who caw in louds.

Here's to robins,
who run—then-stop,
and jays climbing trees:
hop, comma, hop.

Here's to songbirds,
sharp and small.
Hell, here's to birds—
Let's toast them all,

including extinct ones,
a god-awful loss,
and of course the reason
was likely us.

But let's not end there.
It's too sad.
Think of your favorite bird.
Be glad.

∎

Skin-Scanner

As he scans my skin, the dermatologist
talks politics. One of his eyes enlarges
comically behind a magnifying glass.
"Nobody changes Washington D.C.,"
he says, focusing on a small brown
constellation on my wrist. He deems
it "odd but not dangerous." "The most
anyone can do is play the system," he
continues. My body grants

citizenship to new moles every year.
Some are cherry-red. Most are dark brown.
The dermatologist periodically checks
their passports and letters of transit. He's
the Border Patrol of my epidermis.
"The drug companies," he says,
"are raping the system. I can't believe
what they charge for medicine." I'm

naked now before him. He looks
at the scar from a melanoma-excision.
"Looks fine—keep up the good work,"
he says to my leg, which doesn't respond.
All my moles applaud the compliment.
I begin to add items of clothing to my
my mole-crowded body. The scanner

writes notes to himself about
the case of my skin. He presses the pen
hard into the surface of the paper.

■

Skin's Stars

Freckles and moles and other colorations
constellate skin's sky. Imagine connective
lines, then conjure epidermal legends:
huntress of the thigh, magic beetles near
the feet, miraculous bird on the back of
a hand. Or not. Go with the logistical reading,
points on a dermatological map suggesting
deeper strata of DNA, a digital code of
ancient migratory patterns—ah, but also
of collusions with sunlight. *Glory be to God*

wrote Hopkins, *for dappled things*,
and skin qualifies: dot-commissioned
by blots and bits of pigment, uncoalesced
pointillist portrait painted on your body's
parchment, a realistic abstract rendering.
Scars appear like halted asteroids on this
sky, or they try to get a message through
using ghostly notation—something about
the time you fell down on creek-slate or
tried to break up a dogfight with one hand.

■

A Wave in San Diego

A wave begins as a shrug
in the Pacific. Its shape is
a form beginning takes
just before becoming dissolves
into not-any-more. A lovely
curve of water lifts itself and
is carved by its own foamy,
bladed edge. You can't say
for sure the sudsy bubbles
frothing sand a minute later
were ever that wave, nor can
you prove they weren't of
it. You can believe
you remember the wave,
but that belief dissolves. You
can take a picture, or several,
but you will have a picture, or
several, not the wave. Perception
rolls through mind like a wave,
breaks on a shore of forgetting,
and more waves are always coming
until mind ends. Waves of perception
start with a wrinkle in reality,
take and give shape simultaneously,
as when for example you stand looking
at a wave in San Diego.

■

Like a Simile, As a Sign

Briefly astonishing, then gone,
the semiotician vanished like a gray fox
at dusk. Like a tectonic plate,
the structuralist's bowels
shifted. She quaked. Like the moon,
the tides, the sun, and the seasons,
the rhetorician repeated himself
conventionally. As the banker dismissed
the janitor's dignity with a sneer, so
the academic Marxist derided poetry
as bourgeois scribbling, even when
practiced by a welder. As the feminist
lauded the recovery of a lost novel,
so the waitress frowned to see the size
of the gratuity this scholar left. Like
the universe, there is no thing. There
is no thing like the universe.

■

The Compost-Lesson

Aunt Nevada showed me
a compost-heap between
the ranch-house and her garden
when I was 8. I don't remember
what she said. I remember *that*
she said, talking to me as if
I were older than 8. She was trying
to explain how composts worked
and their relation to gardens.

The sounds of her explaining:
these I heard and liked. They
were human noise in a language
I understood. She was an aunt
providing linguistic nutrients
to a nephew. I remember seeing
a cracked white egg-shell
and coffee-grounds in the compost.
I remember a strong compost-
smell—not unpleasant; earth-perfume.
I saw fat red worms writhe
as if they were having bad
worm-dreams. Around the meadow

where the Zergas had built that ranch,
conifer-covered Sierra mountains stood
stately in full sunlight. Wind made leaves
of cornstalks in Aunt Nevada's garden gossip.

■

Evangelical Detour

On the way to deposit
tithes in a secret account,
a preacher lost his way,
found himself misplaced in woods.

Hungry and bug-bitten
beside a creek that smelled
strongly of sewage, this
preacher asked God

to direct him toward
a way out. A weird
child appeared then. There
was something too wise

about her pallid face. There
was no indication she lived
anywhere but in
those woods. Maybe, thought

the preacher, she lives nowhere.
She said to him, "Throw the money
away. Throw it, preacher, in
the creek." He said, "No."

Of course he claimed the money
belonged to God. It wasn't that
the child disagreed. It was that
she smiled thinly, sweetly.

She said, "Then throw it in
the creek, preacher. Throw that cash
in there. Do you doubt God
will retrieve it if it belongs to Him?"

The preacher knew his powers
of conviction had left the congregation
of his mind. He was hungry
and bug-bitten, lost in woods.

He feared the child more
than any lacerating snake.
He flung the money in the creek.
He watched the currency float

on water like leaves. The child
evaporated. The preacher
was tempted to reach for the money,
run after it. In his mind,

he saw it drying on the rocks.
But he turned, and he left.
He woke up in his car. A state
trooper tapped on his window.

"Am I dead?" asked the preacher,
after the window had come down.
The servant of the people said, "No,
sir, but you look like hell."

■

Retired Oracle

Even oracles retire, weary of working
for the future, fed up with telling the truth,
a nasty business. The job-titles embarrass:
*soothsayer, psychic, fortune-teller, card-reader,
prophet, futurist, wizard, statistician, hustler.*
Leaving the cave,

cubicle, or sound-stage for the last time,
the oracle welcomes a future of telling lies,
claiming ignorance, and getting things wrong.
"Things wrong": what a laugh, thinks the oracle—
things are either wrong or about to be.

That's the truth. Some people need an oracle to
tell them so. Home at last, the oracle dreams of
reading history, for who can predict the past?
Books on shelves promise to tell the truth. The
oracle looks at the volumes and needs to
    believe them.

■

For Librarians

Imagine you can consider all ideas
and images represented by all words
and numbers in all libraries worldwide.
Open the book of this consideration.
Touch the paper. See the illustration
of you, reading, when you were ten
in your local library. Turn
several pages. Now read how you
and that other person ignited romance
in, of all places, the stacks, third floor,
in quite a different library. Snowflakes
brushed against dark glass as you two
stood between PQ and PR.

Now go to the index. Find "possibility."
Look up from the book. The librarian
who looks away was watching you.
She knows how to phrase the question
you want answered.

Librarians know where wisdom's stored.
They catalogue the countless forms
of silence and tell people what they
didn't know they wanted to know.
They treat the mentally fractured
as if they're whole, the dull as if they're
sharp, Winter as if it's Summer.

A band of sunlight angled through high
windows brightens shoes of a librarian,
who knows the patron in the gray enormous
coat will steal a book about sex or wiccans.
She knows some Christians will steal books
deemed Satanic, ignoring a commandment

and the homeless person sleeping in a chair.
She knows some atheists treat Library as
Church, so when she moves into shadows,
she does so quietly. She worries for books.

For the librarian knows books are easily burned,
recycled, or digitized, reduced to oxygen, carbon,
silicon, and such basic elements as hate and
budgetary cuts. She
wishes presidents of the United States would
consult librarians before going to war. It would
save so much time, so many lives. She knows
exactly which references know how badly any war will
go and how soon citizens come to loathe their leaders.
She knows how to find stories about all the libraries
wiped out by war. She knows patrons who've been
harmed by war. Sometimes they set off alarms.
Someone asks her, "Can you help me find out
if I'm related to Napoleon? " Yes," she answers,
"come with me, please."
All libraries may now gather inside invisible
electrons. After closing time, books in Sweden
send emails to maps in Chile. A librarian in Topeka
posts a reply to one in Tokyo, adding to
a blue thread wrapped around the globe.

As sincerely as librarians worry for books, for shelves,
for catalogues, buildings, and Best Practices, so should
we worry for librarians, for images and ideas.

At a table in a library, a circle of light
lies on a book. The hand not writing turns
the page, and something important happens.

■

Insurance

Is your abode too close to the river?
Does your home sit astride a fissure
between slabs that uphold illusions
of real estate? Is there a slope
above or below your place
that will one day fall for rain?

Perchance, did you build
a match-factory next to a field
full of dry, oily brush? Well, wherever
you live, your roommate is risk—
statistically. Pay us, please, in case

your relationship with risk becomes
more, or less, than Platonic. Rest
insured. If the river riots or Earth's
complexion cracks, if all falls down
or bursts into blaze, then count

your blessings, muse on ruination,
and wait for our reply. In the meantime,
we'll be watching data gather round
the mean. We'll keep your money

in a vault well away from risk,
from you. We'll keep your money safe,
where it can work in peace for us. If

you should find you need us, well,
let's just see what happens, shall we?

■

Rampant Significance

There's too much meaning. Everywhere
you refuse to turn, something means.
Messages are getting across. Answers
proliferate like dust mites. Typhoons
of information saturate our land.

In my mind I found the image
of a solitary Sumerian slowly
etching text into stone. The notion
of a billion text-messages per
[insert unit here] then swept

the Sumerian and his chisel away like
an ant on a twig in a flash flood. No one
has time to be absurd. People
furiously make themselves understood.
To what end? Points are being stressed.

■

The Clothing

Laundry in a basket still wore
some of sun's expenditure
and breeze's perfume.

Eventually, we put on these
washed things. They led us
back out into sunlight, into
lakes of air. We wear

the repetitions of our days,
dress our bodies with our ways,
fold clothes of our woven
consciousness, put them
in closets of memory, hang
them in dreams, where they
re-costume themselves
in carnivals of synaptic light.

People from an old civilization
called Time sit beside a slow
river, rubbing wet cloth with
stones, paying no attention to
the gods who splash and cavort
nearby, who rise from the river
and cloth themselves in sky.

∎

Any Storm in the Port

The coastline forms a question-mark,
which punctuates the sentence of this day.
From where you live, you cannot see
buildings that display a harbor-view.
No ship docking down there will bring
adventure to your life. Even the cargo,
quotidian as it is, will be shipped elsewhere.

Idly, you wish for strange weather—
hurricane, tsunami, dead-calm, lock-down
fog. This wish would be irresponsible if
linked to a reality outside your head. You'd
never kill an albatross, interrupt a whale's
progress, organize or break a strike. You

are a cove that occasionally dreams
of being a bay. Viking—you might have
been a Viking. -Not a berserker hacking
villagers but a rower who would pull
the boat in a gray unmapped direction
for as long as it took or until you died.
You're that sort—a kind that history never
notices from its panoramic view. You
pull your life through life.

■

Clear a Place For Good

Make room for something good to happen.
Clear a place—there, perhaps, on a purple
divan; or here, on a warm, flat rock. Yes, of

course, nothing good may arrive, in which
case you may occupy the place yourself and
call it good. You may watch as something good

happens in that space you just vacated.
It doesn't always work this way. Still, make
some room. Some room for good.

∎

How to Get Ideas for Poems

It's surprisingly easy. Since you're already in
your mind, even if others claim you're not, just
look around in there and see what's on the
shelves and prairies, in the tunnels and trade-
shows: sharks, appliances, jeans, turnips, primal
scenes. Maybe foaming dog-mouths full of teeth.

Scan acres and vistas of words—native,
transplanted, farmed, found, pilfered, grafted,
milled, mulched. It's a sometimes forgotten
fact that poems are made of words.

Allergies and outrages are good. Grudges, too.
Love? Sure. Why not? Do what you have to do.
You and your mind are already in the world,
in spite of jokes philosophers tell, so you don't
have to make a special trip to peaks, Paris,
bull-fighting rings, deserts, or dance-halls
to find what advertisers call inspiration.

If you want inspiration, just keep breathing.
(If you want anything, just keep breathing.)
The poems will follow. Some ideas will cling
the way stickers stab socks when you walk
through brush and grass. Others will settle—
shadow, soot, silt, and shock. Some will pound
on the mind's door like a drunken neighbor
who came back to the wrong house. Some

will whisper and mumble like spies, gossips,
gamblers, and prophets. Basically, just
let it slip that you're a poet. The news
will get around your mind, and there will be
no end to the ideas. You'll have to
fight them off with poems.

∎

How To Write A Poem

First, clear the area of critics.
Next, grab an image or a supple
length of language and get going.
It's all you now. Mumble, sing,
murmur, rage, rumble, mock,
quote, mimic, denounce, tell,
rock, or tease. Recall, refuse, regret,
reject. Dive, if you dare, into
psychic murk. Down there grab
the slick tail of something quick.
Hold it if you can. Meanwhile,
bellow, bellyache, browbeat,
cry, or call, for all I care. I care.
Invent like the conning, conniving
poet you are, you lying spitter
of literature, you. Make it for
yourself and fit it to you. You
might as well. Readers, editors,
teachers, preachers, profs, and
publishers aren't your friends.
Other poets are busy with their own
poems and problems. Famous poets
are off being remarkable geniuses,
eccentric visionaries, sunken wrecks,
dead, dead-drunk, or pains in the ass.
Say what you see, see what you say,
write it for love and for free. Own what
you write and give it away. Language
will always love you back, so lay a wet kiss
on the words, and when and if in doubt,
remember: what you want to be is to be writing.

∎

Before Katrina

What size, what color, how many?
said the New Orleans T-shirt merchant.

*Say, buddy, jus' a minute, jus'
a minute,* said a drunk man
on Canal Street, his life misplaced

behind his eyes somewhere. *Talk to
you for a minute?* he asked.
Later I stood behind gauze
of hotel drapery looking

at charcoal silhouettes of
financial towers, night. I'd given
the boozy man some money.
To the street-vendor,
I'd said *big, blue,* and *one.*

■

Phantom Pantoum

From the reeds of memory's marsh,
The phantom pantoum speaks itself.
It isn't owned by anyone.
It is composed of gathered sounds.

The phantom pantoum speaks, itself
An act of filling up a page or pause.
It is composed of gathered sounds.
It is a thing that's said and made.

An act of filling up a page or pause
May satisfy the phantom pantoum.
It is a thing that's said and made
But not one, maybe, that's heard or seen.

"May satisfy the phantom pantoum":
That is not a bold assertion,
Nor one, maybe, that's heard and seen.
The phantom pantoum is like a dream.

■

Sonnet in a Bar

I sat beside a sonnet in a bar.
The sonnet looked done in. I bought a round.
The sonnet sipped its rye and said, "Too far.
"I've come too far and lived too long. The sound
Of iambs thumping drives me mad.
And yet if someone called me up on stage,
I'd sing the syllables, and I'd look glad."
"What must a sonnet be?" I asked. "A page,"
The sonnet said, "a one-page hunk of verse.
If you're a poet, then I'm going to scream."
I bought another round. "It is a curse
To be a lyric-form that people deem
Enduring but others try to kill for good.
And—oh: the rhyme I think you'll want is "hood."

■

Molecular Mood

Molecular in nature were the two,
For they were human, and therefore made
Of carbon, protein, fat—the usual stew
Of which stuff in this matter, fact, is said

By scientists to be composed. But how
Does one molecular composite reach
The point at which it loves, the point called Now
Wherein one body-mind, by means of speech,

Decides and then declares this thing called Love,
A concept generated by uncounted other
Molecular composites, the stuff of
Which Civilization's made? Whatever.

The she loves him; the he loves her. Their cells
Conspire to cast reciprocating spells.

■

Salongen och Skogen

By Erik Gustaf Geijer (1783-1847)

Stojande verld, du mig plågar!
Hvar fines stillhet? Dit vill jag vandra.
På allt havad hjertat frågar
Ej får du svar af dig sjelf, ej af andra.

Hellre I skogen jag vankar.
Aftonens flägt genom kronorna susar
Men mina stilla tankar
Hör jag ändå, fastän skogen brusar.

Polite Society Versus The Woods

(translated from the Swedish by Hans Ostrom)

Noisy world, you plague me!
Where is there stillness? I'll go there.
An old heart must not ask
Hard questions of itself or of another.

I'd much rather wander in woods
Than watch days get devoured by official fervor.
My languorous thoughts long
For a forest, listen for its steady murmur.

∎

Critic

She prefers poetry that arrives already
branded with authority, stamped with
approval. Literature is her business,
and business abhors an accident,
such as a wilderness crying in a voice,
or a great poem left anonymously on
someone's doorstep. Anthologies aren't
orphanages, she thinks; they're
consolidations, portable museums, banks.

In photographs of her, bookshelves rise
behind her like battalions, she will not smile,
and she looks ready to retaliate with one
swift blow of erudition should you express
an opinion. Her criticism is like vinyl
siding. It isn't poetry. It isn't necessary.

∎

Door Poem

Some doors are made of wood,
and some of fear.
Inside, you hear
the knocking; wonder: Should

I open up to what I cannot see?
Outside, you knock,
don't try the lock,
think: What, who, might greet me?

∎

Elsewhere

Do you wonder what people are doing Elsewhere?
If you do, then I do. I'm here, which is Elsewhere
to you, who are Elsewhere, too, to me.

I know what people are doing here. Sometimes
it makes me cry. I hold out hope, therefore,
for Elsewhere. I don't know why. I imagine

other, better, things; breathe easily; sigh.
Elsewhere's where we need to meet, I think,
to ask us why we cannot ever get along

right here, where good will seems to die.
Maybe Elsewhere is the place in which our
better selves might resettle to repair

the damage done by tawdry instincts
by and by. I think of Elsewhere, I see,
as a place amenable to possibility.

■

Woman In A Waiting-Room

I guess her age to be 80. She's kept
herself looking the best she can: lean
like a late aunt of mine. The gray
hair's tinted blond but cut
with no-nonsensical reserve—the style's
what they used to call "page-boy."

Trousers, a sweater, sensible beige shoes.
Her back hardly lets her bow to examine
magazine-covers on a table. She squints
and scowls so hawkishly, that I think for a
moment she's spotted a spider. She
selects none of the magazines: wise.

She sits now and looks out western windows,
lifts her face to muted afternoon light,
takes out a compact, and applies red lipstick.
Blue eyes above lightly rouged cheeks look
coolly into the mirror's report. She's not
looking for approval, only information. She
forms her lips as she has done for more
than six decades. Compact and lipstick
disappear. She settles into the chair,
into defiant patience, and waits, newly
painted lips pursed, for her doctor's
nurse to open a door and call her name.

■

Worrisome Quatrain

I like to worry about
things I can't control.
It works as well as eating
from an empty bowl.

∎

August Afternoon

A breeze off Puget Sound curls
around a corner of the abode,
rushes through a line of herbal
foliage—three kinds of mint,
a stout rosemary plant, parsley,
chives, oregano, thyme, and
leathery-leafed sage. The breeze
organizes an aromatic syndicate,
which bargains collectively with
a gardener's sense of smell
on an August afternoon.

■

Horizon

No one can measure the distance to
the horizon, only the distance from it.

The horizon doesn't exist, but it must.

One must determine the place between
high tide and low tide, then measure up

to the point from which one wants to

envisage the horizon, which is a fiction
resting on a line by the angle above sea-

level from which one overlooks ocean. Okay?

There is no fixed point to the horizon,
or to measurement, or to looking at the sea,

or even to living next to the ocean, a notion.

There is a sea, a coast, two tides, a triangle
tied to a plane on a sphere. Let's grant these,

please. There is no horizon, except insofar,

so far, as something seems to end out there
a certain uncertain distance from here. There

is no distance like show-distance to the horizon

because if one travels it, the distance, then
the horizon will have moved away. Still

one is free to measure by the sea. They can't

take that away from thee. One is free to look
and to say, "Look, there's the horizon." Okay?

∎

Strong Views

On the narrow road rising steeply
to Sierra City's cemetery, a
sign advises, "Not A Through Street."

(*No shit.*) We set the headstone of a dead aunt
next to a rock wall her brother, now also
dead, built. We place beneath the concrete

a full bottle of whiskey, a
horseshoe, a deer antler, and
a piece of rose quartz. Otherwise,
the aunt's not represented here
except in our memories. Her
ashes travel up by an alpine
lake somewhere. The family's
idiosyncratic, you might say,

and tardy, even haphazard, with
its burial rituals. In fact, there
are no rituals, no funerals or
formalities. People get together
eventually, share some laughs
and glum grief, eat, and drink.
And laugh more. We're gladly morbid.

A panting black dog lies
in the pickup truck watching us lay
the headstone. Later, the aunt's
two remaining brothers will visit
the stone in the shade, have
a look, say a total of, oh,
seven words, maybe. For now,

we kid around in the cemetery,
get the job done—nobody's god-
damned business but our own, and
if anyone should ask for a permit,
God help them. Goodbye
to Aunt Nevada. The smooth blue
stone, saved from an arastra,
gives the pertinent dates, her
other last name, and a nickname—
then mentions, "Strong Views."

■

Horse-Trail, High Sierra

Riding horses in the High Sierra, we take
trails threaded through hulking conifers,
bypass a Maidu ceremonial hill
covered with black gravel. Breezes off
Gold Lake wrangle scents of wildflowers,
thick aroma of skunk-cabbage, corn-lily,
and a plant that some call mountain misery.
The horses snort thin air. There's sign of bear.

Lightning felled a tree not long ago.
Now new thunder-clouds amass explosive,
creamy ambition over blue distant peaks,
east. Alpine meadows seem closer to
Paradise than most places, at least
in this easy summer's ride. The

sun-scalded cowgirl from Portola
leading the way shifts on the saddle
and hollers unsentimentally, "This
tree you're passing's over 300 years old."

■

Poem By the Side of the Road

Here is a poem that lives
by the side of a road
in the form of a shack
with a tin chimney stack
and a recluse stirring inside.

Walk on the road past
the shack if you will; see fine
dust rise from your foot-fall,
and if you're brave, shout a call
to the recluse stirring inside.

A poem is a shack, and a
shack is a poem, or
so the tautology flows. What's true
of poems and shacks? Who knows?
The recluse stirring inside.

■

Highest Form of Art

"I regard," said the famous novelist,
"tragedy to be the highest form of art."
We were meant gravely to absorb this
highest form of her opinion. One among
us, however, sneezed. Another, a
notorious literalist, believed
a makeshift sculpture on the Himalayas
to be the highest form of art. A
third believed tragedy to be the lowest
form of the raw deal offered by Life.

None of us spoke, though, until later.
We knew enough not to disagree publicly
with a famous, highly paid literary
guest, who seemed to be running a mild
royal fever; who appeared to be slightly
flushed with her current stature,
the highest form of her reputation.

■

A Writer of Parables

Once there was a writer of parables
who aimed to treat his readers'
maladies with narrative caplets
of wisdom. Almost no one read
his parables, for almost no one
read, and those who did read
had many reading choices. The few
who read his parables didn't know
the parables were meant instructively
to heal. They liked the parables,
however, because they were short
and crisp like chopped stalks
of celery. There was the parable
of the blind fashion-photographer;
of the return of the responsible
daughter; of the man who would play
only a rented harp; and so on.
Finally the writer of parables wrote
himself into a parable. He dissolved
into a little bit of his own home-made
wisdom and entered the bloodstream
of culture, completely absorbed.

∎

Fleeting Real

There will always be time to talk
of politics, money, and law. Speak
of one, and you speak of all three.
See the gray cat sitting on a blue chair?
That's where we might begin instead.

We might also speak of hand-carved
spoons, fossils in a dream, or languid
lovers' restless fingers. The rest
is history, a kind of tidied up
lie or a molten sack of evil,
depending upon your point of skew.

When a horse smells lightning,
a millennium's sadness sways.
Let's imbibe words on matters
such as these. The fleeting is
the real, as is a fantasy of
reeling in a moment that glanced
at memory's bait, declined to bite,
and dove to settle in the murk
far below an angler's flaccid geometry.

∎

Bear Nearby

Tonight a bear's at the perimeter,
beyond where cabin-lights dissolve.
The animal breaks brush and gulps air,
snorts, working hard, and we hear this.
We glance up at *Ursa Major* above
the Sierra Buttes, a risen massif.

We figure the bear's breaking down
an apple tree now and gorging—wild
and deliberate, focused and irascible.
We don't walk closer. The bear doesn't
advance. There's a distance to be kept.

There's a fascination in the dark,
which entertains a big invisible mammal
whose family's lived here since before
any human named constellations or
eavesdropped on night's business.

∎

Moon-Shot 1969: The Missing Article

Somewhere between the moon and the Sierra Nevada, our TV-reception got fizzed. We leaned in toward the Zenith set that labored to freight us images of Armstrong. Outside, illusory sky still pretended to be blue. " . . .one small step for man, one giant leap for mankind," said the Zenith, and I knew the first man on the moon had flubbed prefabricated lines. The article "a" was missing, and without it, "man" and "mankind" meant pretty much the same thing in 1969. The article

"a" is still missing. It tumbles in the Milky Way, silent in an unspoken vacuum. Yes, yes, I was properly amazed like everyone else. And a little sad. After a cumbersome astronaut stepped off a ladder and set feet, the moon misplaced its mythology and became dirt and destination.

■

Man In A Hole

In summer's citified humidity, one man
pierced a street's asphalt hide with a
jack-hammer. Then someone else in a yellow
back-hoe dug something like a grave. Soon
another man was standing in the hole. Orange
plastic cones stood sentry around him. He
wore a white hard-hat and an orange vest.
Cars passed thickly by on both sides, hauling
their noise, puffing exhaust-fumes, hardly
slowing down. The man's height had been cut
in half. His co-workers looked down at him
expectantly, as if he could fix anything—
sewer, water, electricity, earthquakes.
"People give me shit," he yelled, "and
    I'm tired of it!"

■

Sestina: The Game of Baseball

The circle is the center of the game:
The trip from home to home; mound; ball.
And Baseball's creed is O-penness: fields;
Gloves, bird's mouths; past fences lies forever.
The game plays out in formulae of three.
Combinations interlock like rings.

Grave umpires speak in prophecy that rings
Out in the voice of Moses. *Out, Strike, Ball*
Mean really *Shame, Yes, No!* The game
Is subtle, though, like its faintly sloping fields.
And indefinite: A game can last forever
In theory, infinitely tied at 3 to 3.

Though rules say nine may play, it's often three
Who improvise a play within the game.
(Tinkers, Evers, Chance). Pitcher lends ball
To air. Potentiality of bat rings
With power in that instance. All fields
Beckon to innocence and hope forever.

One chance at a time drops from forever.
Player with a caged face grabs for ball.
But batter knocks ball back into the ring
Of readiness, at which point one of three
Things happen that can happen in the game:
Safe or Out or Ball-Beyond-All-Fields:

Home run. Inspire the ball past finite fields,
And you voyage honored on the sea that rings
The inner island. Sail home, touch three
White islands, Hero. Gamers since forever
Have tried to sail past limits of the game,
Shed physics' laws, hold Knowledge like a ball.

To know this game you have to know the ball,
An atom when contrasted with green fields—
Less than orange, white with pinched rings
Of stitches ridged for grip. With ball come three
Clear tasks: throw, catch, bat. These are forever
Of the Circle in the Center of the Game.

Dropped in the fluid game, the solid ball
Starts widening rings of chance, concentric threes
That open out into the Field. Baseball. Forever.

∎

Memo From November 6th Street

They make it work somehow in Memphis,
bluff buttressed against an oceanic
river. Vines overwhelm scruffy trees,
weariness overtakes work, and Downtown
pines for its heyday. You know the story:
Handy, Rufus, B.B., Elvis, Booker T.
& 'nem fused grooves like welders
building barges bound for big water.
They made it work somehow.

Sir, ma'am, if you want to, you can
sit in a black iron chair next to where
Johnny & June Cash and Ella wrote their
names in cee-ment. Pigeons and a goat
will stare down at you as you stare up
at a plastic palm tree & you'll drop money
into a yellow bucket, sit back down,
and listen to covers of Albert King,
Robert Johnson, Stevie Ray Vaughn,
Son House, and Otis Redding. *Looks like
nothing's gonna change* in Memphis.
Then it does. Then it doesn't. They
have to dredge the channel regularly.

Meanwhile I have to check out the Just
Like New consignment-store on November 6th
Street—Memphis, yes, sir: Memphis—caught
in a corner between Arkansas and Mississippi,
between St. Louis and New Orleans, mid-South.
They make it work somehow. Somehow they make it.

∎

Memphis Monologue

No, sir, I'm not from
Memphis. I'm from New
Orleans, but I came
to Memphis after the
Hurricane. There was
nothing left for me
down there. Been here
ever since, but it's
tough. I haven't been
able to find much work-
the economy; and all.
If you like barbecue,
you might try the
Rendezvous. You have
a good evening, sir.

∎

Adjustment Denied

The man from the Building
came to adjust the Psychiatrist's
thermostat. He called the Doctor
from the Waiting Room. The electrons
of his voice spoke to those of
Voice Mail. He left a Message.
"I am from the Building. I have
come to adjust your thermostat. I
am in the Waiting Room." Beyond
the barrier of messaging, there
was no Answer. Air, however,
spoke in a constant whisper
through the ducting of the
Building, as the Doctor, so
the man from the Building guessed,
talked and listened to a Patient
in an Office which was too Cool,
too Warm, who knows?

∎

A Little Something That Refrains

Let's write a little something that refrains
From trying to be more than poetry.
The language moving in a poem obtains.

For language is an actor, plays and feigns,
And hopes we'll see what it wants us to see.
Let's write a little something that refrains

Itself in lyric and won't grab for gains,
But is content simply to seem and be
The language, moving. In a poem, "obtains"

Can take an object or refuse. The lanes
Of speech form labyrinths. Let's drink some tea.
Let's write a little. Something that refrains

Might well refresh. The mind's eye strains
Relentlessly, desires profundity.
The language moving in a poem obtains:

It's there like creeks and rivulets from rains.
Word-lovers lap up language happily.
Let's write a little something that refrains.
The language moving in a poem obtains.

∎

Because Comparisons Matter

Leaving aside a summer's day, what
would you like to be compared to?
A winter's night? A rhino's hoof? A
traffic jam in Athens, Toronto, or
Beijing? You tell us. At

Comparative Poetry Enterprises (CPE),
LLC, we try to satisfy the subject
of our poetry. Our philosophy is
that good market-research leads to
good poetic analogies. No disrespect
to Shakespeare, but times have changed.

The poetry-market is tough, especially
in the Analogy and Love sectors, which
have been saturated. We're CPE: dedicated
to making the right comparison for you.
Contact us for a free, no-obligation
trial-poem. You'll be glad you did!
CPE . . . where comparisons are incomparable.

∎

The Time-Drunk

"I got out of bed last night to go to the bathroom, and I started walking backwards. Strange things happen when you get old."
 —Passenger on the Amtrak Cascade train

"Beyond a black hole's gravitational border–or event horizon–neither matter nor light can escape."
 —Discovery.com

He got drunk on time, toxed with sips
of minutes, gulps of years, dregs of
decades. Now he staggers down alleys
of memory behind Chronology's moist
row of pubs, saloons, clubs, and dives.

A lifelong drinker of time, he knows
how drunk he is but not where. Surfaces
bump him, rough him up. Gravity trips
him using cobblestones and curbs. He
finds a door he thinks he recognizes,

enters a noise, finds the bar, orders
a wee timetail. The one behind the bar
refuses, judges, speaks the savage,
polite words, "You've already had enough.
I can pour you a cup of coffee, though,

or call you The Cab." He assumes
the false dignity of a confronted
tippler. He mumbles, "The Cab." Waiting,
he negotiates. To the one behind
the bar, he says, "Come on. One more?"

■

Chardin's *Still Life With Fish*

I've noticed how, in Jean-Siméon Chardin's
*Still Life with Fish, Vegetables, Gougères,
Pots, and Cruets*, the paint becomes
Plexiglass because it seals off odors
I seek. Or should I say "aromas"—odors
formally attired? Chardin's

manipulation of pigment teases me
with an imaginary robust stench of
French kitchens, dead cool slimy fish
hanging above vegetables and such.
Chardin invites me to the unstill
kitchen, then closes the glass door

firmly, and I'm left with an inedible,
unsniffable scene. Well done, *monsieur,*
to taunt the nose of an olfactory voyeur
in the deep-freeze of an art gallery.

∎

If I Were A Werewolf

If I were a werewolf, I'd know
where werewolves live. Most
must hail and howl from
imagination, I imagine, but some
might come from some place
outside the town of Lore.

Were I a werewolf, how would I behave?
Hirsutely, rudely, carnivoraciously?
I guess so, but maybe less so
than cinema would have it. Perhaps
I'd chiefly want to be alone,

denned up on some steppes, serenading
the loony moon, napping and scratching
like any other mammal. Or maybe
werewolves run in packs like lawyers,
politicians, and beer, in which case

I might have to have a role, a niche,
a boss, a pledge of loyalty, a werewolf
oath or anthem—the usual frightening
stuff that makes the atavistic hair
on the back of the neck rise up.

∎

Celebrity Author

I think I know what the celebrity-author was
thinking: *Get me out of here.* He wore
fame like a hair-shirt. The thing is, the money
is great, adulation's like liquor, and it's nice
to be thought a genius. So there he was, and
there we were. . . .

He squirms and fidgets. He goes on too long
and comments on his commenting like a daft
monarch. He doesn't like other people's wit
because it shows everybody's witty and fame
is more arbitrary than not. Of course,

we'd all trade places with him in the Land
of Hypothetica, especially because we'll never
have to. He won the lottery, he's a good writer,
and there's a wider justice in his fame. Still,

he itches and scratches, poses and opines,
tries to say shocking things, grins guiltily,
reminds us of his fame and wit and money
at paced intervals, and suspects what he
knows to be true: that we, too, can't wait
for the evening to be over.

■

His Photos Were Not His

The temporary celebrity wasn't celibate. He deleted from "his" hard drive photos of himself and others frolicking in "privacy." Digital piracy ensued. A Dickensian clerk at the local rag-and-computer-parts recycling shop recognized the fellow and reconstituted images from the celeb's impersonal computer, sold them, and they enjoyed a viral notoriety on screens around our sad and rocky globe.

The celeb and his publicist met the media and were quoted. The clerk got fired and paid a fine. There is no line. No one owns anything: prophets have murmured this news to us over eras. Now the Internet has made their knowledge common. *Intellectual property* and *private photos* languish in the Oxymoronic Lounge, sipping mocktails next to an irrelevant highway. The celeb should have hammered the hard drive with a sledge, but paparazzi would have clicked a thousand images of that, so there you go, and so it goes.

■

Oakland Is There, Baby

Gertrude Stein famously said a lot of famous
things fashioned to be famously remembered
tenderly such as, of Oakland, California, U.S.A.,
"there's no there there," but after she left
and eventually went to Thereville, France,
the There of Oakland that had actually always
been There remained There in her absence.

See, Oakland had and has persons, places,
and things—the stuff that composes the There
of any place from Paris to Bangkok, Vladivostok
to Lesotho, Aberdeen to Montevideo. Gertrude
wanted more, or less (who knows?) from Oakland.
—Some irony to that since she possessed the Oak-
landish visage of a stevedore or boxing
promoter, a face with angles and planes in which Picas-
so found a lot of There to paint in
the portrait he painted.

Gertrude wrote some inlandish Oaklandese
sentences and hit some of them right on the
button, and then she died. Oakland's still there.
Who are more alike than Gertrude Stein
and Al Davis? Both willed their wills on art
and sport. Oakland's There was there all along,
and will be, and is, is there, and there you have it.

■

Old Seagull

One old white seagull prowled wet grass
near brick buildings, looking for worms.
It walked arthritically and seemed chilled.

A lone, hunched seagull is a dignified
defeat, a sign of how hopeless hope is.
Was the bird's eyesight still good enough

to see worms? Did the bird ache? Do
seagulls fly back to the beach to die,
or do they get stranded on a street,

eaten by a crow or a raccoon? The
seagull was a general in exile,
a feathered Napoleon on Elba.

It was a heroic nun, a white flag
hanging from a wall of a blasted fort.
The gull seemed to know everything.

It kept its routine of life.
Walking past, I admired the bird,
which ignored me, which I admired.

■

Rhinoceros

Evolution left rhinoceros holding
a heavy load, freighted down with
muscle, bone, horns, and heft, all
held up by four short legs.

Rhino, you're an envoi from dinosaurs.
People are your predators, as ubiquitous
as sunlight, as shifty as shadow,
lethal and silly: grinding your horn
into powder? How fucking stupid is that?
I like the way you stare

sadly straight down the tunnel of
history. I like that rough-hewn
stone spike you carry on your face
but would never want to own it.

Let hummingbirds be nuanced. Some
creatures need to be as subtle
as an avalanche. Big leathery
rhino, you're among these, and not
that your large ears will process
this word as meant, but *Thanks.*

∎

About Hobbema's Landscape

(Meindert Hobbema, 1638-1709)

Hobbema's "A Wooded Landscape with Travelers
on a Path through a Hamlet": clouds, trees, and
shadows overwhelm people and buildings.

Even a patch of sunlight, mid-painting, might
be ominous, a precursor to thunderstorm.
Villages, hamlets, and no-account small
towns live on the edge of being devoured,

one way or another. They are beside nature's
point—are one tornado, flood, avalanche, or
economic downturn away from obliteration. I'm
sure Hobbema had something else in mind with

these pigments, the tracks left by
his traveling strokes. I like how he knew
foliage, clouds, and shadow lord over a mere
hamlet made of brick and milled wood.

∎

Towards Evening

The muted roar of tidal surge
sounds like a convergence of one
million whispers.

Reflection of the sun's unrolled
like a ragged carpet on the surface
of the sea.

To touch the wind with your tongue
is to taste ancient salt and conjure
braids of kelp.

Soon the sea will say its vespers
deep inside its tidal whispers.

■

Small Garden

When carrots come up, they're green hairs
on Earth's loamy pate. Already, though, they're
pointing covert orange fingers toward Earth's
molten core. Carrots like cool weather. Tomato-
plants don't and therefore hunker. They hold
out for the blaze, in which they'll then sprawl
promiscuously and weigh themselves up
with serious loads of red. That said, lettuce
is the lovely one, presenting delicate textiles
of itself to sun. So goes growth in post-Edenic
gardens, fallen and common, full of manure
and worms. They're seedy, sketchy, weedy, vetchy,
half-cultivated, half-rude, all vulgar. Water and
weed, heed the almanac, fill a sack or
two at harvest time: all to the good.

■

The River Moved

I get used to watching rivers move from up
to down. Then someone will remind me,
"The river used to be here until it moved,"
and I picture rivers walking slowly across
plains, opening another canyon for themselves,
going underground for a spell, or running into
dams—nibbled by turbines and turned into
a lake that sits and waits but never loses
its desire to find a sea. The way rivers move's
a note slowly written in cursive to time, whose
mail historians and geologists open. For instance
the famous river-boat that sank's buried on a dry
plain now because the big river moved. "It's just a
grave now," someone said. "Bones are down there,
remember. No one wants to dig."

■

Spuds

Potatoes grow out of potatoes like an
underground dynasty while the rest
of agriculture bustles above-ground
with blossoms, pods, and fruits.
Potatoes multiply themselves in sequestered
arithmetic. They send up gestures
of leaves to appease sunlight. Meanwhile,
they populate their tomb, glow inwardly,
will stand for harvest or sit tight—possess
a kind of divine patience, an honest secrecy.

Spuds aren't glamorous, decorative,
geometric, or vibrant. They're lumpy,
plain, idiosyncratic, and common. They
get along with rocks, advise moles, ignore
frost, and huddle in carbohydrate caucuses.

■

No Strings Attached

He told her he preferred a relationship
with no strings attached. She said she preferred
strings attached. For instance, she wore an anklet
woven of string. Sometimes she kept her hair back
with a simple elastic circle of string. Her clothes were
made of threads, a kind of string. And, she added, she
preferred to keep her clothes on at least for the immediate future. She

said that if he and she were to take a long
walk into a relationship, she would want
to tie bits of string to branches so she'd know
the way out for sure in case they got lost.

He said, "It's just an expression." "You mean
like 'string of words'?" she asked. "It means,"
he said, "I'm not your puppet and you're not
mine. It means 'no commitment'." She said,
"Your shoe's untied." He looked down. It
was untied. She wasn't kidding. He knelt
to tie the string of the shoe. When he arose,
he saw that she'd vanished, no strings attached.

■

Mongrel

Our operatives have determined he's
not worth our operatives' time.
He's anti-social but polite. He has problems
with authority but a Puritan's work-ethic.
He's a well-traveled, well-read hick. And
he's extremely loyal but can't grasp
the concept, *patriotism*. Alas, he's

a hot-tempered pacifist and a cloistered
utilitarian. He's often observed in the company
of anarchists, contrarians, the shunned,
the shy, the maladjusted, and the eccentric.

He is not to be trusted unless he's your friend.
He's jaded and guileless, optimistic, morose,
habitual, and unpredictable. He is by turns
too loud and too quiet. Our operatives,
who do a lot of listening and watching,
report he does a lot of listening
and watching. These latter are his most
worrisome traits, but our operatives
have determined he's no threat to the State.

■

Employee

No matter how long, how well,
you work for us, you're only
as good as your health is today.

We're not sorry to say
that to us what we pay
you is overhead.

Yes, your record is good,
but alas, it describes a past
from which we've made a

profit already. We're a
forward-looking company,
as we mention in our

annual report. Yes,
experience counts,
but our calculations

show inexperience to be
cheaper. Thanks. We hope
you've set a little something

aside. Our size is downed.
Your time is up. We wish you
luck (one more lie for old time's sake).

■

Lyric Craving

Sometimes I crave a lyric poem
That springs like a clear creek,
A regulated rush of words
To wash a weary week.

A yellow butterfly in air,
A jet-trail frozen high:
Such images are welcome, too.
They fill the lyric eye.

In Housman and in Dickinson;
In Langston; Auden, too.
There's often something sharp and quick.
The words are right and few.

I'll go read these, and others, too:
The Spare Ones, let us say.
I'll sip the water from the creek
And slake the thirst today.

∎

Venues

My residences are three—
the present, past, and me.
The past is vast, illusory.
Present's cramped, a tiny pill,
so its contents spill
into the past. Still
there's Me, which is a what
that's a where and a who,
and not so different from a You.

■

Rhododendrons Without A Country

Rhododendrons in Canada and the U.S.
may be aware of a lot, but they don't know
they're Canadian or American. They're
even undecided about whether to be trees
or shrubs. Unsurprisingly, then, they bloom
cautiously. Vivid swatches of color peek
through grenade-size buds and give Spring
a good hard look to see if it's serious or
a double-agent working for Winter.

Rhododendrons never carry a passport
or negotiate treaties. They're model
citizens of forests, parks, and gardens.
Their leaves are leathery, seem wise.
Rhododendrons conduct business with
sun, soil, and rain. They exhibit a
cosmopolitan poise that rises
above petty nationalism.

■

For Cafeteria Workers

The task of cafeterias is to feed
many people quickly. Cafeterias aren't
so different, then, from farms and ranches,
except the clientele is often
less polite than cattle, horses, and pigs.

Back there in the kitchen, they get it
done, the workers: Soup for thousands,
noodles for hundreds, protein and starch—
all timed to be there when a herd arrives
with bad moods and lots of opinions.

The dish-room's a symphony of clash,
a humidity of food-smell, steam, and sweat,
a silver cacophony. The conveyor-belt's
the boss. Each tray might serve catastrophe.

The automatic dishwasher—a tunnel of water
and soap—disgorges disinfected implements
eaters will soon stuff in their mouths again.
The pot-washer is a lonely figure. Once I was
he. Heaps of stainless steel arise, food welded
to metal, grease smeared on every plane. Alone,
you work your way through the mountain 'til
nothing's left but you, your soaked shirt, and
clocking-out. Out front, the servers smile.

They remember names and endure whiners
and would-be gourmands. Runners fill machines
that distribute fizz and syrup. Cashiers stand on
weary feet and process armies packing trays,
hunger, haste, and attitude. Bless the cafeteria
workers, who are better than we deserve.

■

Watching Bach Played

I saw a string-ensemble play
Bach's music. Each musician
leaned, turned, and swayed
in chairs differently as
they played. The women's
backs looked strong in gowns.
The men's feet in black shoes
stayed fixed to shiny floor.

Sometimes violin-bows poked
straight up as if probing unseen
clouds just above the players'
heads. Portly cellos had to be
held up like friendly drunks.
They mumbled low genial
gratitude. One man stood

above the players, waving
his arms and a stick as if
to try to get someone's
attention. The violinists
may have glanced at him,
I don't know, but mostly
they cuddled their polished
wooden instruments, and
let their bodies feel the music.

■

The Ambitionator

Climb into the Ambitionator. Hear it
power up. Strap yourself in. Adjust
the goggles. On the screen, see your
dreams come true. Feel the force
of being in charge. Hear the acclaim.

Oops, time to power down. No,
I'm afraid it's just a ride. Yes,
you have to get out. No, you're
not anyone special. That's why
the ride feels so good. Yes,
you'd have to get in line again,
buy a ticket. If I were you, I'd
find a cafe, sit down, and be
obscure and you. The Ambitionator

is just a ride, my friend. You're
nobody in a carnival. I'm nobody
who works in one. This, my friend,
is the strangest ride of all, our lives.

■

The Fallibility Sonnet

My fallibility has tripped me up
Again. I've fallen on the gravelly ground
Of imperfection. I would like to cut
This nonsense out, but no; my flaws have found

A way to find me even when I seem
To have evaded them successfully.
They just show up and are a well trained team—
And venerable. Yes, some have been with me

So long, I look at them with a strange mix
Of loathing, dread, familiarity.
Of course I have some antidotal tricks
And textual guides. Spirituality

Assists. Self-admonition, too.
Regret. I sigh. But still: what's one to do?

■

Notes in Five Paragraphs on How to Write an Essay

According to my notes, an essay
should have a niece's statement,
which is different from a tropical
sentence. An essay should have a
beginning (how could it not?), a
middle (seems easy enough), and
an end (unlike time, which is infinite).

An essay needs evidence. Otherwise,
the perp walks. The essay's exertions,
if my notes are right, need supporting
retail. Paragraphs require transmissions,
and the paragraph-brakes need to work.

An essay should have an interesting title,
such as "The Duke of Windsor" or
"Vampire Vixen." The essay should not
include any logical phalluses. It should have
a good sense of its audience, even though
no one will ever actually pay to see the essay
perform in public. Oh—and it should be

grammatically erect, I am told, and it should
impose a sin-tax on its sentences. There
shouldn't be any coma-splices or
spit-infinitives. Obviously, nobody wants
an essay to induce a coma or project saliva.

An essay must sight its sources on a "Works Sighted" page. The essay should be engaged to its reader, but that sounds kind of creepy to me. In conclusion, these are my notes on how to write an essay.

■

They Say About A Poem

Technically a poem ought to have words
in it although a blank page beneath a
title's mighty inviting, a bit like a
snowy meadow after a day filled with
looking at city crowds. They say
about a poem that a poem should show,
not tell, and be, not mean, but others
think a poem should tow, not sell,
and, really, how can a poem that *is*
not *be*, and why can't it mean while
it's being? From poems people crave
imagery, they say, they say about
a poem, but actually all
the imagery's in their heads, put there

by literacy's reflexive response to
letters applied to a surface such
as paper or a surface such as plastic
or indeed an ear's membrane. Should
a poem have conflict? Opinions about
that bicker. I know a poem that featured
many quiet rooms where you could go to get
away from all that conflict in plays,
life, novels, factories, politics,
and movies—where you might listen

to a clock chime and watch the weird
butler straighten ancient paintings
on the walls of your personality, but
I guess that, too, is a conflict.

■

Walk in the Sunshine

How should I walk in the sunshine?
—Winter's been so long, the sun
so seemingly distracted.
My shadow will come back
and stick to my feet. Also,
I'll need to get used to moving
and being glad at the same time.

"It will come back to you," people
say. They say, "You'll remember how
to walk in the sunshine." They don't
know this. Nothing comes back. We
make up memories, ask questions,
and behave as if we're points of reference.
And did I tell you about the avalanche?

That's re-routed everything around here.
Anyway, the upcoming interval doesn't
know some people call it Spring and everybody
calls it something or other. Time reflects
not on its own situation. Time is completely

unselfconscious, unaware that it seems
to stalk us constantly. Time's always constant,
in spite of Relativity. No questions occur to
time. Nothing. It knows how to walk
in the light of every star.

■

Crossing the Creek

They wait for me across the creek.
They look like shadows from this side.
One day I'll wade across to seek
The insubstantial. Petrified

With cold and fear, I'll stand, midstream,
And feel what's real: round, slippery stones,
The force of water in a seam
Of that ravine. My skin and bones

Will read the creek a final time,
Will feel its push and temperature.
I'll stand unsteadily, a mime
Without an audience and most unsure

About the balance of the act.
But then I'll move, make it across.
The creek will be the final fact—
Its gravel, boulders, trout, and moss.

The far side shall be near. I'll fall
Into the life of death. Will they assist,
Who've gone before, and bear the pall
When I fade into a mottled mist?

■

In One Quiet Room

In one quiet room, your life occurs,
not in avenues, halls, or fields. You're
born in one quiet room. In another,
you love. In another, grieve. In one

quiet room, you'll face a final suffering
and die. Yet you may dream of conquering,
of wielding power vastly beyond just
one quiet room. You may become

enthralled with self, indulge in self-
coronation, delude yourself into seeing
a castle and a realm in one quiet room.
Pretend, pretend. Life will rein you in,

return you to modest proportions,
four measured walls, a bed, a light,
a table. If you are blessed, there will
be some who love you at the end.

They'll tend to you in one quiet room
where your small life will end with
struggling breath and final yearnings,
morphine, and transport of soul.

In quiet rooms that may seem full
of noise and business, our life occurs.
Consider that tonight as you consider
friends who come and go in one quiet room.

■

Evening Hatch

An evening hatch of gnats rose from the river
in a cloud. One gnat flew to a blue bluff,
landed there, pushed against infinite,
immovable stone mass. The gnat

fell away and down toward a pool,
out of which erupted a rainbow trout,
which snatched and swallowed the gnat.

I will have had less effect on things than
this gnat. It's good to meditate on that.

∎

Still Surprised

I'm still surprised crickets can make
that noise. With their legs. Still surprised
by literature, by love, by eyes. Still
surprised when societies function.
Astonished still by cruelty. Mystified
yet by existence's existence. Always
shocked by violence. I'm still surprised

by the pull of words. Still puzzled that
a part of me imagines it can bring back
those who died: magical thinking. Still
flummoxed by what, exactly, the roles
of child and parent require. Remain

wounded, permanently altered, by
the murders of JFK, Malcolm X, MLK,
RFK, Allende, Palme, Till, Biko, and all
the so-called nameless ones. Still
stunned by numbers attached
to people killed. One. Ten. One
hundred thousand. Forty-five thousand.
Six million. Twenty-five million. I'm still
here, so it seems, surprisingly. I'm still
surprised I'm surprised by cynicism and lies.

■

Intimacy

through gap in drapes she and he
see light of streetlamps brightened
by snow. they know the scene without
seeing it – pretty – if you're not in
the scene and still trying to get
somewhere if not home. they feel
heat of their bodies commingle naked
partly under covers. he inhales smell
of her hair as if it were a rare perfume.
it is. she savors her alertness to the feel
of his arms easily on/around her body,
a gentle, safe weight. this, this time
they occupy, is a now and a before.
this is intimacy, where ecstasy incubates.
she and he, breathing noisefully, wordless,
know one will say something soon. neither
knows which one or which words. maybe
a movement, slight, will decide. languid
anticipation of what will be thrilling
thrills even as neither yet stirs, the light
made brighter by snow filling the brief
gap between drapes.

∎

The Extravagance and Reticence of Love

The extravagance of love desires
to discover continents and patrol
seas. The reticence of love desires
one kiss, one sniff of the beloved's
magical breath, sweet and metallic.

The extravagance of love manufactures
metaphors the way nations churn out
weapons. The reticence of love searches
for the one thing to say that will make
the beloved laugh, an authentic giggle
from the belly, the tender abdomen,
a holy place. The extravagance of love

makes vast promises, plans trips to
Argentina, and compares the beloved
to condors and catastrophes. The reticence
of love takes off its clothes and sits
in the dark until the beloved says something
to advance the quest. The extravagance

of love yearns to be as simple as reticent
touch, and the reticence of love wants
to be a colonel who owns acres of poppies
and pastures of horses. Reticence

and extravagance meet as bodies meet. They
disappear into a particular moment, and all
is frenzy, and all is peace, and all is well.

■

Into the Folds of It

Into the folds of it, we fold
the night over us. Into the swells
of it, we sail, feeling the rock
and the ride of this invisible boat.
Tasting the rain, salty rain
from the sea, we rise from
an undersea dream, we meet,
and we ride the sweet storm,
the curves and hollows.
We see the pinks, brown, and reds
of the coral, the reef of our
meeting at night, holding each
other in the ache of the darkness,
in the want of the waves going
into the folds of it, folding it
over as we come to the shore.

■

INDEX OF FIRST LINES

A breeze off Puget Sound curls 81
A civil liberty might be defined 39
A politician's head swelled. 20
A student asks some simple questions. 14
A wave begins as a shrug 55
According to my notes, an essay 126
After the moon has set but before sunrise. 22
Although we've never met 10
An evening hatch of gnats rose from the river. 132
As he scans my skin, the dermatologist 53
Aunt Nevada showed me 57
Briefly astonishing, then gone,. 56
Climb into the Ambitionator. Hear it 124
Do you wonder what people are doing Elsewhere? . . 78
Electrons here, electrons there, but no 40
Even oracles retire, weary of working 60
Evolution left rhinoceros holding 110
First of all, what an unusual term. Second,. 26
First, clear the area of critics. 70
Fold night several times until 34
Freckles and moles and other colorations 54
From the reeds of memory's marsh, ... 72
Gertrude Stein famously said a lot of famous 108
Go as you wish into that good night. 33
He got drunk on time, toxed with sips 102
He told her he preferred a relationship 116
Here is a poem that lives 87
Here's to starlings. 52
Hobbema's "A Wooded Landscape 111

How should I walk in the sunshine? 129

I get used to watching rivers move from up 114

I guess her age to be 80. She's kept 79

I hate to break this news to me: 43

I like to worry about. 80

I live in wariness, ... 44

"I regard," said the famous novelist, ... 88

I sat beside a sonnet in a bar. 73

I saw a string-ensemble play. 123

I think I know what the celebrity author was. 106

I'm feeling sorry for yourself 9

I'm still surprised crickets can make 133

I've noticed how, in Jean-Siméon Chardin's 104

If I am in your book, then thanks 25

If I were a werewolf, I'd know 105

If we add up all that we claim to know, ... 42

Imagine you can consider all ideas 61

In El Greco's Christ on the Cross, earth 51

In one quiet room, your life occurs, ... 131

In summer's citified humidity, one man 93

In this wet city under gray today 17

Into the folds of it, we fold. 136

Irish Girl sat on a crate. 35

Is your abode too close to the river? 63

It's surprisingly easy. Since you're already 68

Labor breaks you. When you're young, ... 16

Laundry in a basket still wore 65

Leaving aside a summer's day, what 101

Let's lay down some lines for Langston 49

Let's write a little something that refrains.	100
Make room for something good to happen.	67
Molecular in nature were the two,	74
My fallibility has tripped me up	125
My residences are three—	120
No matter how long, how well	118
No one can measure the distance to	82
No, sir, I'm not from	98
Noisy world, you plague me!.	75
"Oh father, dear father,	45
On the narrow road rising steeply.	84
On the way to deposit.	58
Once someone advised me to run	12
Once there was a writer of parables	89
One old white seagull prowled wet grass.	109
Our operatives have determined he's.	117
People we see once: flood of faces, coats,	36
Potatoes grow out of potatoes like an	115
Rhododendrons in Canada and the U.S.	121
Riding horses in the High Sierra, we take	86
She prefers poetry that arrives already	76
So is light particle or wave.	18
Some doors are made of wood,	77
Sometimes I crave a lyric poem	119
Somewhere between the moon and the Sierra	92
Stojande verld, du mig plågar!	75
Technically a poem ought to have words	128
The circle is the center of the game:	94
The coastline forms a question-mark	66

The extravagance of love desires. 135

The gratification can be extreme. That's true. 28

The headline from the Sacramento Bee 46

The man from the building 99

The mountains round that town are sheer. 48

The muted roar of tidal surge. 112

The task of cafeterias is to feed 122

The temporary celebrity wasn't celibate. He 107

The things I don't remember. 15

The villain, L, disrupts this life of ours. 38

There was a place where people lived a long, ... 41

There will always be time to talk 90

There's nothing spherical about the space. 50

There's too much meaning. Everywhere 64

They make it work somehow in Memphis, ... 96

They wait for me across the creek. 130

through gap in drapes, she and he. 134

To be human is to sit cross-legged 24

Tonight a bear's on the perimeter. 91

What size, what color, how many?. 71

When carrots come up, they're green hairs 113

When the tongue 27

Wherever you enter the story. 21

Index of Titles

A Little Something That Refrains 100
A Wave in San Diego 55
A Writer of Parables 89
About Hobbema's Landscape 111
Adjustment Denied 99
Any Storm in the Port 66
August Afternoon 81
Ballad of the Micro-Town 48
Bear Nearby 91
Because Comparisons Matter 101
Before Katrina 71
Blogosonnet 50
Celebrity Author 106
Channel-Crossing 35
Chardin's *Still Life With Fish* 104
Chocolate 22
Civil Liberties Sonnet 39
Clear a Place for Good 67
Cosmic Status 42
Critic 76
Crossing the Creek 130
Crushing Fate 12
Democracy Today 20
Dice 34
Door Poem 77
Duke Ellington 46
El Greco's *Christ on the Cross* 51

Elsewhere 78
Employee 118
Evangelical Detour.. 58
Evening Hatch 132
Fleeting Real 90
For Librarians 61
For Cafeteria Workers 122
For the Birds 52
Go As You Wish 33
Highest Form of Art 88
His Photos Were Not His 107
Horizon 82
Horse-Trail, High Sierra 86
How to Get Ideas for Poems 68
How to Write a Poem 70
Human in an Airport 24
Idiosynchronized 36
If I Were a Werewolf 105
In One Quiet Room 131
Insurance... 63
Intimacy 134
Into the Folds of It 136
Labor Breaks.. 16
Langston Hughes and Barack Obama 49
Light Verse 18
Like a Simile, As a Sign 56
Lyric Craving 119
Man in a Hole 93
Sestina: The Game of Baseball 94

Memo From November 6th Street 96
Memphis Monologue 98
Mere Sympathy 9
Message From A Bookmark. 25
Modernist Shame 14
Molecular Mood 74
Mongrel 117
Moon-Shot 1969: the Missing Article 92
No Strings Attached 116
Nostalgia for Nothing 15
Notes in Five Paragraphs
  on How to Write an Essay 126
Novel: A Sonnet. 41
Nub of the Matter. 43
Oakland Is There 108
Of Photosynthesis 21
Oh Ballad, Dear Ballad. 45
Old Seagull 109
Only Dreaming 17
Phantom Pantoum 72
Poem by the Side of the Road 87
Polite Society Versus the Woods 75
Quantum Sonnet 40
Rampant Significance. 64
Retired Oracle 60
Rhinoceros 110
Rhododendrons Without a Country 121
Salongen och Skogen. 75
Sexual Orientation 26

Skin's Stars 54
Skin-Scanner 53
Small Garden 113
Sonnet in a Bar 73
Spuds 115
Still Surprised 133
Strong Views 84
The Ambitionator 124
The Clothing 65
The Compost-Lesson 57
The Cunnilingus Poem 28
The Extravagance and Reticence of Love 135
The Fallibility Sonnet 125
The River Moved 114
The Time-Drunk 102
They Say About a Poem 128
Towards Evening 112
Transaction 10
Venues 120
Villanelle: The Villain, L 38
Walk in the Sunshine 129
Wary Lyric 44
Watching Bach Played 123
When the Tongue 27
Woman in a Waiting-Room 79
Worrisome Quatrain 80

About the Author

Hans Ostrom grew up in Sierra City, a small town in the Sierra Nevada mountain range of California. He graduated from Roseville High School and attended Sierra College. He earned a B.A., M.A., and Ph.D. in English at the University of California, Davis. Since 1983, he has taught rhetoric, creative writing, and literature at the University of Puget Sound, a small college in Tacoma, Washington. As a Fulbright Senior Lecturer, he taught at Uppsala University in Sweden. He also taught at Johannes Gutenberg University in Mainz, Germany. He is married to Jacquelyn Bacon Ostrom. Spencer Ostrom is their son.

Hans Ostrom's previous books of poetry are *Subjects Apprehended* and *The Coast Starlight: Collected Poems 1976-2006*. With Wendy Bishop, he also published the chapbook, *Water's Night*.

He has also published three novels: *Three to Get Ready, Honoring Juanita*, and *Without One*.

Since the late 1970s, Ostrom's poetry and short fiction have appeared in a variety of magazines and anthologies, including *Blue Collar Review, California Quarterly, Commonweal, Cutbank, In Tahoma's Shadow, Journal of the American Medical Association,*

(continued)

Kiss Off: Poems to Set You Free, Ploughshares, Poetry Motel, Poetry Northwest, Poetry Nottingham, South Carolina Review, South Dakota Review, Spoon River Quarterly, The Washington Post, and *Xavier Review*.

He has published essays and book-chapters on teaching writing, and, with Wendy Bishop and Katherine Haake, he wrote *Metro: Journeys in Creative Writing*, a textbook for creative-writing. He also produced *Lives and Moments: An Introduction to Short Fiction*.

Ostrom's criticism and scholarship include two books about the work of Langston Hughes. With J. David Macey, he edited *The Greenwood Encyclopedia of African American Literature* in 5 volumes.

Ostrom is Professor of African American Studies and English at the University of Puget Sound, where he was awarded the President's Award for Outstanding Teaching. He has also worked as a carpenter's assistant, a hod-carrier, a dish-washer, and a journalist.

Other Books by Hans Ostrom

Without One: A Novel (2011)

Nine By Three: Stories. With Beverly Conner and Ann Putnam. Introduction by Ronald R. Thomas (2011)

Honoring Juanita: A Novel (2010)

The Coast Starlight: Collected Poems 1976-2006 (2006)

The Greenwood Encyclopedia of African American Studies. 5 volumes. Edited with J. David Macey (2005)

A Langston Hughes Encyclopedia (2001)

Metro: Journeys in Writing Creatively (2000)

www.ingramcontent.com/pod-product-compliance
Lightning Source LLC
Chambersburg PA
CBHW031358040426
42444CB00005B/333